Death of a Polaroid
A Manics Family Album

Death of a Polaroid
A Manics Family Album

ff

faber and faber

Contributors

—

Nicky Wire

Nicky is the bass player and
lyricist with Manic Street
Preachers. The group have released
ten critically acclaimed albums
over two decades, during which time
they have won — amongst others —
four Brits, an Ivor Novello, five
Q awards, the *Mojo* Maverick award
and the *NME*'s coveted Godlike
Genius Award.

manicstreetpreachers.com

—

Mitch Ikeda

Japanese photographer and long-term
Manics collaborator Mitch Ikeda
first shot the group for *Rockin' On*
magazine in 1992. In 2002, Mitch
published *Forever Delayed*, a
collection of his studio and
documentary photos of the group
over the years. At times he has
kept Manic Street Preachers on the
road thanks to his unparalleled
skill as a trained masseur.

mitchikeda.com

—

Jeremy Deller

British artist Jeremy Deller has
produced two collections inspired
by Manic Street Preachers as well
as several films for the group. He
was the recipient of the 2004 Turner
Prize and in 2009 he received the
Albert Medal from the Royal Society
of Arts. *Unconvention* – the
collection he curated at the Cardiff
Centre for the Visual Arts in 1999
– was the first time artworks by the
likes of Warhol, Bacon or Picasso
had been hung in Wales.

jeremydeller.org

—

Robin Turner

Robin is a writer and editor.
He has DJed regularly at Manic
Street Preachers gigs since 1996
and written extensively for the
group's website.

robinturnerwriting.wordpress.com

—

Farrow

Farrow is a London-based graphic
design studio. They have worked
with the Manics on albums including
Everything Must Go, *This is My
Truth Tell Me Yours* and *Lifeblood*,
as well as designing Mitch Ikeda's
Forever Delayed.

farrowdesign.com

First published in 2011
by Faber and Faber Limited
Bloomsbury House,
74-77 Great Russell Street,
London WC1B 3DA

Design and art direction:
Farrow

Polaroids photographed by John Ross

Printed in China by C&C Offset
Printing Co. Ltd

Photographs:
049–380 © Mitch Ikeda, 2011
381–553 © Nicky Wire, 2011

Foreword and Commentary:
© Nicky Wire, 2011

Polaroids, Politics and Folk Art:
© Robin Turner, 2011

Book design:
© Farrow, 2011

The rights of Nicky Wire to be
identified as author of this work
has been asserted in accordance
with Section 77 of the Copyright,
Designs and Patents Act 1988

A CIP record for this book is
available from the British Library

ISBN 978-0-571-27852-7 (HBK)
ISBN 978-0-571-27853-4 (Special Edn)
ISBN 978-0-571-27854-1 (Limited Edn)

Every effort has been made to trace
or contact all copyright holders.
The publishers would be pleased to
rectify any omissions or errors
brought to their notice at the
earliest opportunity

10 9 8 7 6 5 4 3 2 1

Dedicated to Jim Fletcher

Contents

Foreword
Nicky Wire

As is so often the case with art – whether music, film, photography or painting - true beauty shines through in the imperfections. In a pre-digital age, the representation of 'the moment' – unplanned randomness caused by the restrictions of the format – was often what made artworks so captivating. The hiss as analogue tape ran through reel-to-reel machines. The warmth of a proper live room with decades' worth of stories to tell. The flicker and crackle of Super 8 film through a handheld camera. Or the magic of watching a picture develop in your hand. We live in an age now where anything can be retouched or remixed; where Photoshop or Pro Tools can fix everything that wasn't quite right on the day, where you can buy an app for your phone that can replicate any photo style you want at that time; where, basically, you can cheat at anything. To me, the Polaroid has always been a truly honest format. I'm sure it's one of the reasons I've been utterly fascinated with them since childhood.

There is no truer representation of 'the moment' than the Polaroid. I would never describe myself as a photographer, but I've been addicted to Polaroid pictures for as long as I can remember. They played a vital part in documenting the magical moments of my youth and they've been a constant in documenting the history of Manic Street Preachers. When the band started, every photo session began with a Polaroid; before long I began taking them myself to record the world as I saw it; trying to find beauty in humdrum days off when on tour or during downtime in the studio. As a band, we used Polaroids on sleeves around the time of *This Is My Truth, Tell Me Yours*. Each of the singles from the album contained a reproduced Polaroid; the idea being that each would feel like opening a gift – receiving an invite to a secret society even.

During the nineties our long-term collaborator/photographer Mitch Ikeda spent a lot of time capturing us on tour, making records, videos and just being ourselves as bandmates and friends. Even though the pictures in this book by him are the work of a professional, they still retain the spontaneity and romance that a classic Polaroid shot always should.

When the photographer started a photo session with a test Polaroid, I would always ask to have one as a memento. I find these shots – by the likes of Rankin, Kevin Cummins, Tom Sheehan, Steve Gullick – particularly revealing as you can see four people becoming the band. Every time we did a session in those days, we became Manic Street Preachers.

For me, the Polaroid is the perfect medium. With time, colours fade and lines blur but the details of lives caught on camera in that split second are always genuine, honest and truthful.

Nicky Wire
May 2011

Polaroids, Politics and Folk Art
Nicky Wire and Jeremy Deller

In conversation with Robin Turner

Turner Prize-winning artist Jeremy Deller has worked with Manic Street Preachers on numerous occasions over the last two decades. In many ways, their respective careers have run in parallel – outsider status followed by the embrace of the mainstream without any compromise or dilution. This conversation on art, music, politics and the working relationship between the two took place on a balmy spring morning in a London hotel room.

When did you each become aware of each other's work?

NW I was thinking about this the other day; I think it would have been the T-shirts.

JD It might have been the T-shirt that Richey bought from the shop I worked in (Sign of the Times in Covent Garden – the shop also promoted parties). It was printed with a Philip Larkin quote. I didn't know he'd bought it until I saw it in *Select* Magazine. I was a shop boy back in the early nineties and I'd made a bunch of shirts to sell. Ones with slogans taken from tabloids, things that said 'My Booze Hell', 'My Drug Shame' . . . ones with mod targets on the boobs. Courtney Love bought one; Robbie Williams wore one in his last appearance with Take That back then.

NW That's a good threesome – Courtney, Robbie and Richey. Nothing in common at all there!

JD I'd seen the band before that though; I'd seen you playing at the Marquee supporting a band called The Throbs.

NW That was an amazing gig.

JD You smashed all your instruments up at the end. Me and a mate went along because we'd heard the main band were supposed to be the next Guns N' Roses. We knew we'd never get the chance to see the proper, early days Guns N' Roses, we were too late, so we went to see the Throbs on the off chance that they might be a good substitute. And they were terrible.

So even though you were working at the heart of acid house, you were secretly loving G N' R?

JD It's a myth about me that I was

The Uses of Literacy
Jeremy Deller, 1997
Pencil on paper, pen on paper,
books, collage on paper,
photographs, acrylic on canvas.
Dimensions variable

AUSTRALIA
ENOLA ALONE
FASTER
FROM DESPAIR TO WHERE
GIRL WHO WANTED TO BE GOD
KEVIN CARTER
LA TRISTESSE
LITTLE BABY NOTHING
M*A*S*H
MOTORCYCLE EMPTINESS
MOTOWN JUNK
NO SURFACE ALL FEELING
SMALL BLACK FLOWERS
RAINDROPS KEEP FALLING
ELVIS IMPERSONATOR
STAY BEAUTIFUL
FURTHER AWAY
A DESIGN FOR LIFE
YOU LOVE US

The Uses of Literacy
Jeremy Deller, 1997
Publication

The Uses of Literacy
Jeremy Deller, 1997
Collage by Stephanie Cross

someone who used to go out, take Ecstasy and dance all night. I was really into the scene but I was never a big joiner-inner. I wasn't someone who was going out to big raves – they kind of scared me. And I loved metal. I went through a very intense heavy metal phase in my twenties. Probably far too late really!

NW Is that what drew you to us maybe? The fact that we talked about G N' R so much in the early days?

JD Guns were almost a pop band. I remember the first time I heard 'Sweet Child o'Mine' I couldn't believe it. Like the first time I heard 'Smells Like Teen Spirit'. I was at a baggy indie nightclub; I heard it at two in the morning very loud. I remember thinking, 'Oh God, this is the end of this. The Mock Turtles don't stand a chance.' So initially I was very upset with Nirvana for destroying baggy.

NW I felt the same. I remember when I first saw Nirvana; initially I just didn't get them. They had quite an aggressive, male look. I also knew it was going to flamethrower everything. The whole thing went so quickly, no one involved expected it. I was reading a piece about them saying that even after half a million record sales in the States, Kurt Cobain was still sleeping in the back of a car. They weren't preordained by the industry at all. Of course it became apparent pretty quickly that Nirvana were undiluted genius.

—

NW So when did *The Uses of Literacy*[1] come about?

JD 1996. That's when I started writing letters to fans and giving out flyers at gigs.

What had you seen that made you think, 'these people are worth investigating'?

JD I knew about the Manics' avid fanbase and I found the whole thing intriguing. I've always loved artworks made by fans about their idols. And I knew that it was very rare that you got to see things like that. I just wanted to see it – I knew there was a creative scene around the band and I wanted to peer behind the veil of secrecy. I'd seen fanzines and that was as close as an outsider could get to the unofficial folk art culture around the band. The easiest way to sate my desire was to try to get in touch with the fans that were making it and do a show based on it. I still know some of the people I got in touch with back then. The exhibition I put together was only supposed to be on for one day in a gallery in Norwich. I thought it was a great opportunity to stage something.

So this was around the time of Everything Must Go . . .

JD I loved that album so much; it was a really great and very intelligent rock record. A really amazing record that was clever, that had great songs . . .

NW For us it was that magnificent point where we went from the underground to the overground. It's like your Turner Prize year, underground cult concern and then suddenly you're famous. For a band, it's the best moment you can possibly have. And, brilliantly, it can only happen once in a career. Whether you're The Cure or New Order or The Smiths or Muse, if you're the biggest cult band in your country and you have the opportunity to just tip over into the mainstream.

JD I used to play *Everything Must Go* in the shop all the time.

NW Some of the images in that book are just fucking amazing. The one where I turn very slowly into Christ . . . I just love it so much.

JD That whole collection – all those pieces together – it's all owned by the Arts Council now.

NW I didn't know that!

JD They bought the whole thing. They treat it now like anything else in their collection, a Lucian Freud or Francis Bacon. I love that.

NW The other picture I loved from the *Uses of Literacy* book was the picture of me, James and Sean promoting *The Holy Bible* when Richey was in hospital. It was originally from *Sky* Magazine. Whoever did it added musical chords and structures all around us . . . It just looks beautiful.

JD I honestly don't know whether that world has gone now, whether the Internet has killed it, whether people don't sit and draw or collage like that any more.

In a pre-Internet age that must have been a wonderful piece of detective work to undertake, sending out letters and waiting for the replies to come back.

JD And you got tons because word got out. I'd made these little dayglo flyers and gave them out in the queues to the people who looked most likely. You recognise the hardcore fans easily – mainly because they're the ones waiting in line seven hours before the doors open! Very commendable behaviour. That kind of fandom is almost a religious thing, it's a pilgrimage.

NW I think that only really happens with pop acts now, I don't think there's been a rock'n'roll act for years now who've appealed in that way.

You've each become award-winners without compromising the nature of your art (Turner Prize, RSA medal, Brits, Ivor Novellos) – does that acceptance affect art?

NW I think it was easy for us to deal with mainly because, from the start, all we were obsessed with was being huge. We were unashamed in our ambitions. One listen to *Generation Terrorists* will tell you we weren't setting out to be an art rock band. One of our early quotes was, 'The most alternative thing we can do is be massive.' We thought being mainstream was the most subversive thing we could do. At the time we emerged, there was such an indie ghetto and that was definitely something that we were reacting vehemently against. We talked a lot about records like *Born in the USA* by Bruce Springsteen, about how subversive that record was – much more so than say a Smiths record – simply because of the scale it impacted on. So I don't think success has ever impinged on our artistic output. I remember when we won the Brits and we played 'A Design for Life' there, it just felt empowering. Getting up on stage, talking about comprehensive schools and boxers. I never saw winning – standing on that stage, being accepted, as it were – as a compromise.

JD If you win an art award, you automatically become part of the establishment. The good thing is that you can use that to your own advantage. So potentially you can become more subversive through that acceptance, you can slip things in that you might not ordinarily be able to get away with. I try not to think about it too much – I try not to think about what I do too much really. I try not to analyse. Or even read about my work if I can avoid it. One thing I have noticed is that you start getting invited to do strange things. I'm doing something at the moment that involves me hanging round with Michael Portillo.

NW He's one of my favourite broadcasters. As a politician he was completely awful. Now, though . . . *Great Railway Journeys*, *This Week*, his documentary on the Spanish Civil War . . .

JD People love him in the street. I asked him if it had ever been a problem, whether there was a time when he couldn't walk down the street. He said that only twice had he ever been attacked or had unpleasant situations. I was quite shocked at how few times it was really.

NW When he lost his seat it was loaded with so much symbolism.

JD I've been working with him as part of a museums prize. There's a bunch of us going round judging museum restorations. It's the kind of thing you end up doing after you've won art awards. No one pays you but you end up hanging round with people like Michael Portillo . . . And he wears the most interesting clothes. And his hair is a work of art; it's like a sculpture. People are always having their picture taken with him.

—

NW When did you start investigating folk art?

JD In a way, *The Uses of Literacy* was a precursor to the Folk Art collection.[2] It was teenage folk art really. Me and my mate Alan [Kane, Deller's long-time collaborator] were sat in the pub in 1999 talking about the Millennium Dome. I remember saying, 'I bet it won't have all the things we love about Britain in there.' So we started to write

Folk Archive
Jeremy Deller & Alan Kane
Exhibition, Palais de Tokyo, Paris, 2008. Including a retrospective of Ed Hall banners.

Folk Archive
Jeremy Deller & Alan Kane
Notthing Hill Carnival, 2003

[1] *The Uses of Literacy* (1997) was a group show curated by Jeremy Deller comprised of fan-made Manic Street Preachers artwork. The collection is now owned by the Arts Council.

[2] *Folk Archive* (2005) was a touring exhibition made up of work from untrained artists put together by Jeremy Deller and Alan Kane. The collection is now owned by the British Council.

Found That Soul,
Jeremy Deller, 2004
Music video stills

out this list of all the truly great examples of folk art that we'd like to see in the Dome. And they weren't in there. So we decided that we'd put together a collection that would tour Britain that would be about the creative life of Britain, about the things that people actually make and create, what they get up to. It was as simple as that.

NW So do you think folk art was something in your DNA?

JD I've always loved church fêtes and local carnivals, processions. It was something I was brought up to love. My parents were heavily involved in the Church of England; there were always jumble sales and fêtes to visit, every summer would be a succession of things to do. I've always been a lover of community activity.

NW My parents unwittingly pushed me in a folk art direction too. They had a huge collection of Polaroids. My mum and dad took hundreds and hundreds of Polaroids of the family when we were growing up, playing cricket, football, holidays . . . the light on a Welsh beach . . . it's all there, full of joy and beauty.

JD Is that where your obsession comes from?

NW Definitely. We pored through those books – my mum would get them out when anyone came round. Looking at those pictures, I really think that the format is akin to folk art. The photos in the book touch on that idea too, the pictures are scratchy, it's messy. Mitch's pictures are covered in scribbles. He took literally thousands of pictures of us during the three years he travelled with us. The hardest thing was trying to edit them down to a workable amount. I also used to collect all the Polaroids from photoshoots we were doing with the *NME* and *Melody Maker*. There's the first *NME* shoot that Kevin Cummins did, Steve Gullick's picture of me and Richey body-painted for *Gold Against the Soul*, Rankin's *Everything Must Go*. Lots of first-take versions of pictures that people might know. The obsession harks back to my mum and dad. And probably the reason I was so keen to pick up those pictures from our photo shoots

back then too.

JD So you had this love of Polaroids ingrained then. It's magic for a kid to see the process that those pictures go through as well.

NW It's a touch of genuine magic. As Polaroid has stopped producing, there's an added poignancy to the whole project. When I heard it was going, I stockpiled as many films as I could. Just this last week, I used my last roll taking pictures of the family. I do think that in some way there's that connection between us. I'd never have known about folk art without you, even though I'd always felt it.

JD I definitely believe it's something that's ingrained in all of us. You can see it in this country's ongoing love of festivals and getting together, doing stuff.

NW Going back, I do think awards are harder on artists than musicians. With us, it doesn't really mean anything. With a record, you're only as good as your last release. You're not going to get a Glastonbury headline slot based on what's on your ornament shelf back home. In art, it does seem to offer an added cachet.

JD Some artists who win big prizes like the Turner – I'm not going to name names – but some people end up having nervous breakdowns afterwards. It's often much more complicated to win an award than not to win it.

—

I was looking at people who'd used Polaroid as an artistic medium. Warhol was quoting as saying that he loved the camera because, 'It made people look just right.' There's other examples – Allen Ruppersberg, David Hockney . . . Ringo obviously . . .

NW Tim Roth, who was on the cover of *Postcards from a Young Man*, obviously he's holding a camera on the cover of the record. I didn't realise when we cleared use of the picture that he's got a collection of thousands of Polaroid photos. He was obsessed with them in the nineties. That fluky colliding of ideas and events, that creative serendipity it's a very Greil Marcus/*Lipstick Traces* sort of thing. And it keeps happening. James, Richey and Sean's first gig was Echo & the Bunnymen at Bristol Colston Hall, twenty-five years later Ian McCulloch is singing on a Manics track in our studio in Cardiff . . . We went from watching Kylie in *Neighbours* to wanting her to sing on 'Little Baby Nothing', then we end up writing songs for her a few years down the line . . . And strangest of all I got asked to write the foreword for a reprint of *Lipstick Traces*!

JD Greil Marcus is a bit of a genius at those things, isn't he? Like so many people of his generation, he's obsessed with Dylan, who I see as an ongoing artwork. How much can you trash your heritage and still get people fawning over you. You have to view it like that really. Do you know that book *The People's Music* by Ian MacDonald? He writes a lot about Dylan. There's a brilliant essay in it about Brian Wilson losing his mind. He's extremely anti LSD. Very anti drugs in general.

NW I've got to say we were always like that. I can honestly say that I've never taken anything stronger than a paracetamol in my life. I remember when Richey had his first spliff, it nearly split the band up. It was a real code breaker in the back of the bus.

JD Especially that drug, it seems wrapped up in so many things . . .

NW . . . fucking tie-dye, idiots talking shit to you . . . it summed up everything we fucking hated. If it had been speed, we'd probably have been OK with it, that just seems that much more acceptable as a punk-rock drug.

NW Putting together a band archive, I was looking at the video you directed for 'Found That Soul' the other day, it really is fucking mega.

JD The subtext was supposed to be a secret reading club for young women in the future. People weren't allowed to read in public so they would meet in private in darkened rooms to read – we were trying to make reading look sexy and dangerous, which it is. I remember shooting you in rehearsal and Sony very kindly lent us this super-snazzy night-vision camera to work with.

And the guy using it ballsed it all up. We looked back at it and there was a time code whacked right across your faces through the whole thing. No one read the manual so we hardly ended up with any footage at all.

So you shot that and the introduction to the Reading Festival headline slot?

JD Yes, I did the Karl Marx film for Reading. Also some live visuals of insects that we used for 'Masses Against the Classes'; they were really amazing.

—

JD Did you share your interest in art with Richey and the others when you were growing up?

NW Our first ever trip outside the UK as a band was to Oslo and the first thing we did was head to the Munch museum. We did share influences but I think I was particularly interested. Certain things on the *South Bank Show* really got to me. The Francis Bacon one . . . an *Arena* programme on Pollock . . . Willem de Kooning (inspiration for the *Everything Must Go* track 'Interiors') . . . I know it sounds like entry-level stuff but really good telly – especially back in the early eighties – could be so powerful. It was unbelievably inspiring. Also Ceri Richards, Picasso, Kyffin Williams, Kokoschka and obviously Jenny Saville. There was the same impact with writers and poets too. R. S. Thomas, T. S. Eliot, Ginsberg, Plath, Stevie Smith . . . I remember a programme on Larkin when he died that had a massive effect on me. I've never made any bones about the fact that television was the greatest tool in my education. It's taught me so much. I saw one on Hockney back then and I didn't get it. In later life though, I've changed opinion completely. Now I think he's an absolute chap. Going back to the question though, I think my interest in art led in a roundabout way to *Unconvention*,[3] which – even though it's all your doing – is still to this day one of the things I've been proudest to have been involved in. I've never been to anything that has fulfilled me more.

JD Well, thank you. I did try to curate an exhibition from the

Reading Festival Film, Jeremy Deller, 2001 *Video still*

[3] *Unconvention* (1999) was a multi-artist exhibition curated by Jeremy Deller that ran at the Centre for Visual Arts in Cardiff.

Manic Street Preachers fans at *Unconvention*, Cardiff, 1999

Arthur Scargill speaking at *Unconvention*, Cardiff, 1999

perspective of a teenage boy, a fan of things – that was projecting what I thought you and the band would like, really. It wasn't difficult because I think you had very similar tastes to mine at that age. The curator for the show was very tenacious in getting the loans – he would not take no for an answer from the Tate.

NW There had never been a Picasso in Wales up to that point.

JD That came from the Tate, as did a large Warhol and – I think – a Munch. Possibly a Francis Bacon too. We got mega-paintings from them, it really was quite staggering. I can't believe they let us do it too – that museum wasn't even open when they agreed to lend them. Thinking about it, someone could do a very lavish art fraud based on that. Pretend to run a museum and ask for loans for a non-existent show.

NW The gallery space didn't last the year after that. They had a serious problem after *Unconvention* finished its run in that they just didn't know what to do in there.

JD In my opinion it was the kind of art that you shouldn't have to pay to see. That's not putting any of the art down. Images like the ones shown at *Unconvention* are an education; you shouldn't have to pay to see them in London, in Wales, wherever really.

Jeremy – a question – do you know if there were any Polaroids in Unconvention?

JD No, alas – plenty of photos but no Polaroids.

NW It was event art, a destination exhibition. Every time you'd go, there would be at least five kids in feather boas on a pilgrimage. I paid every time, must have gone a dozen times during the course of its run. I just wanted to bask in the glow of what was on the walls, to feel inspired in a city that I love.

JD It's still one of the best things I've ever done. I often start projects with a view that it'll be one way and it never is. I'm sure it's the same with making records. With that, what happened was exactly as good as I thought it could be. It fulfilled all

expectations, which is very unusual for me. There were very few compromises made there.

NW I think for most people in the arts, the fully realised project is such a rare occurrence. So were you becoming a force as an artist at that point? When you were calling people to talk about it, were people taking you seriously?

JD I was working through the Centre for the Visual Arts so they were doing all the heavy lifting. They were the ones calling up asking if they could borrow a Warhol or a Kippenberger. At that point I was known but not on any major level. The first thing that people really noticed was *The Battle of Orgreave*[4] in 2001. *Unconvention* was put together in 1999.

NW We really were on such a hot streak then. We'd had Jenny Saville give us the image for the front of *The Holy Bible*, the designer Raf Simons was putting together Manics inspired clothing ranges, all the Kippenbergers for the singles off that album (*Flying Tanga Part 4* for 'Faster', *Nice Communist Woman* for 'Revo l' and *Tits, Towers, Tortellini* for 'She is Suffering'), you come along and start doing that. It's pretty fucking amazing. There weren't really any other bands around that time trying to project anything other than an insular image of themselves on to the outside world. The Kippenberger stuff was so perfect. And we got it for next to nothing. The sleeve for 'Faster' just superb.

JD What is that song actually about?

NW Well. I wrote about a quarter of it. It was my title and I wrote some of it but Richey was obviously on a roll around then. We talked a lot about it being about the acceleration of culture. That idea seems so odd and antiquated to think about now when you know how the world has accelerated since he disappeared. It was a summation of all the data that was speeding through his head.

How do you think he'd have dealt with the Internet?

NW It's a staggering thought, isn't it? He'd either have rejected it outright or would now stand as the most followed Twitter account in the world. He never had a computer, he used to carry his portable typewriter round everywhere with him. It should be in a museum somewhere. They call it a portable, it's the exact same thing as a normal one just with a fucking lid and handle on but it's beautiful all the same.

—

The Miners' Strike plays a key part in each of your work. Jeremy's first major public artwork was the re-enactment of the Battle of Orgreave while each of the Manics grew up in its shadow in the Valleys . . .

NW The first song we ever wrote was called 'Aftermath'; that was directly about the Miners' Strike. That was in 1986, our fifth year at school. It was fucking awful, admittedly, but it was there like a fresh wound. We were living in the thick of it. I'm not trying to say our childhoods weren't great; it's just that each day you were exposed to conflict between fellow workers and the police. The whole area became genuinely violent; the whole area is an enclave of pits. Or used to be. Rhondda was the last one to go back; I can really remember the parade when they went back to work . . .

JD A mass of banners, brass bands . . . I remember that very clearly. Personally, I just watched it from the TV. Living in the south of England, I received it second hand. At the time it was very clear that something terrible was going on in Britain, even to a sixteen-year-old doing their A levels. I couldn't really do anything about it back then; but it always stuck with me. The whole of that time I was paranoid that any minute we'd be blown up and that the world would end. There was a *Panorama* in the mid eighties talking about what would happen should a nuclear bomb go off in London. They were putting 'Protect and Survive' leaflets through the door; I'd be walking round the house trying to work out the best places to hide. My dad worked for the council and was meant to be given a place in a bunker somewhere, which he said he'd never go to.

NW I remember my dad talking about building a bunker in the garden.

You could have rehearsed in it.

JD I know it sounds ridiculous. It's very difficult to explain to people now that all-encompassing fear of nuclear war. I remember at the time you had war, the Miners' Strike and then AIDS. It was like the Horsemen of the Apocalypse, one after the other!

How did a recreation of Orgreave form as an idea? From an outside perspective, it looks an insanely ambitious project for a young artist to pull off . . .

JD It's kind of comedic as well; there was almost something absurd about doing it. I had this idea about British history and our heritage, about ways of juxtaposing things. And I came up with the idea of recreating the battle with people who do military re-enactments; dressing them up as miners. I wanted to do something sensibly and I wanted something that would talk about British history and how we see war. And I wanted to present the Miners' Strike as a civil war rather than a labour dispute, as that's what I believe it was – the last great civil war, the last proper battles on British soil. It was really simple really. You might have to explain it to twenty-year-old art students but people our age understand it.

NW I can see why that's the case. This is a simplistic way of looking at it but back then, there were loads of fucking hard-working blokes in an industrial sense. A ready army almost. Now they're all working in call centres or driving taxis if they're lucky. Back then there really was a different mentality; there was clearly a certain violence in the job. If you were a steel worker or a miner, you were stood up all day beating things. I don't know if there's an industrial side that can mobilise any more.

I wanted to ask about Adrian Street, the Valleys-born glam-rock wrestler from the early seventies. I know you've worked with him – I was thinking that he represented the ultimate juxtaposition of glam and grit – a quintessential Manics image really.

JD I made a film with Adrian last year. He's from Brynmawr and he's an incredible force of nature. The picture of him at the pithead

The Battle of Orgreave,
Jeremy Deller, 2001
Video stills

4 *The Battle of Orgreave* (2001) was an artwork based around the 1984 confrontation between police and picketing miners that became one of the pivotal moments in the Miners' Strike. The re-enactment was filmed for British television.

with his dad really is the quintessential image of post-war British life, from heavy industry to service industry. When I saw it, I thought it was such a shocking image. Adrian has done amazing things in his life. He was down the pit at fifteen, getting beaten up every day because he had long hair and was into bodybuilding and body culture. His dad used to beat him. They hated each other. That's why in the picture, his dad's face is close to disgust. The other guys in the picture, they're the people who used to pin him down in the pit and cut his hair off him, beat him up. So at fifteen he thought, 'Fuck this' and buggered off to London. And he didn't go back until that picture, by which time he was a famous wrestler. He went back specifically to show them – they were peasants as far as he was concerned. To him, it's a really vindictive image. To the observer, it's quite funny in a way. To him though it's to prove a point, it's cathartic. He's reinvented his life, his looks, everything about himself. I'm sure he's like a lot of people in that profession in that his life is all about him – it's all about the moment, about what he has become. Such a fascinating person.

NW   I wanted to ask about the Turner Prize, about whether you had that comedown moment . . . I'm thinking of what hit us post *This Is My Truth* and the Millennium Stadium gig . . . the Knebworth moment. Did you get a 'what the fuck do I do now?' moment?

JD   I did actually but I've never really talked about it. For about a year afterwards, I was thinking everyone was looking at me. I mean literally and metaphorically. I thought what if I can't do anything, what am I going to do? And I eventually got over it – mainly because someone else wins it the following year and the pressure's off. I was definitely the poorest artist to ever win the Turner Prize, I know that. I wasn't earning any real money before winning. But there was definitely a moment of thinking, 'Oh God, what do I do now?'

NW   That moment is the reason we ended up with Cuba [5]. We wanted a different angle, we were thinking how do you top what's

been so brilliant? You have to think of something gigantic, which is probably the wrong way to approach things . . .

JD   You do things in order to get attention, but for the work not the person, which I know is a bit delusional. I don't particularly enjoy people knowing who I am or knowing my business. Unless it's Salma Hayek! The prize was an insight into how people – especially rock stars – get very paranoid after success. Everyone knows you and you haven't got a clue who they are.

NW   Whatever bands say, most of them – the good ones anyway – are deeply ambitious to beat other bands. I'm fucking terrible for it. Competition is good sometimes, whether it's the Beatles and the Stones or The Pistols and The Clash. You try to outwit yourself and it can go horribly wrong. It's why I defer to sport now, I can put my competitive side into that – someone else can win or fail for me.

JD   It can eat away at you, that jealousy. It's supposed to fade as you get older though, isn't it . . . ?

NW   Hasn't happened to me . . .

JD   So it's keeping you on your toes then. What you said about outwitting yourself as well as others I think is true, if you can surprise yourself . . . actually I'm beginning to sound like a motivational speaker . . .

One last thing. Jeremy: how influential is music over your art? Same question flipped to Nicky.

NW   Visual art is still a massive influence on my writing. At the moment, Dash Snow's Polaroids are triggering off loads of ideas. A picture – whether something like Guernica for example – can end up providing such a great amount of inspiration it becomes hard to explain really. I wrote a song for my solo record named 'Memory Bucket' after Jeremy's Turner Prize film. 'To Repel Ghosts' was a title taken from a Basquiat painting, 'Door to the River' from de Kooning. 'La Tristesse Durera' was famously the last line of Van Gogh's suicide note. I think the visual arts – along with poetry – are probably my greatest inspiration. Some art you understand immediately, some you have to view in an abstract way, which works for me as it means I don't have to contextualise it like every other fucking thing in my life.

JD There's such a pressure to give everything a label. Often it's nice to just be washed away by something.

NW I remember seeing an interview with Howard Hodgkin and he was talking about how the thickness of the paint can inspire you and it's so right. I paint really badly, but at home I've got about a hundred canvases I've worked on. I won't call them works of art because they aren't – I'm not interested in showing them to anyone, but they make me feel good.

JD Painting is fantastic therapy.

NW I remember when Richey disappeared, I just painted non-stop for months. I didn't write any lyrics until 'A Design for Life'. I've got all these horrible, anguished paintings that sum up the emotion of the time. Now I love painting, getting messy, getting the kids involved . . .

JD Well, that's what so much good art is – playing around. As for music on my art, obviously lots of the subject matter central to my work is related to music, directly or indirectly. My first major art experience as a child was watching *Top of the Pops*. This was when music was arguably at its most visual with glam rock, which not only sounded incredible, it looked amazing too. That was definitely one of the key influences in my life. I've always been very interested in how music looks. I can't play an instrument so there's no way I could ever have been in a band. I always longed to be in a band but for a few good reasons that never happened. I'm always drawn to documentaries about how terrible it is to be in a band – the Ramones one (*End of the Century*) is so tragic, so amazing. All those films about the misery of being in a band, I'm obsessed with them. So, it's natural for me to do things around music, it's always been a cornerstone of my life. That said, I don't really listen to music much any more. I don't

really find myself moving far beyond Radio 4.

NW I'm sort of the same. Travel is the one time I dedicate to music. I used to hate travel. A twelve-hour flight to Japan, Sean loads the iPod up and I'm fucking cock-a-hoop.

JD I went to a 'young persons' gig' recently and I couldn't help draw parallels with the past, thinking they were Devo. It's terrible to start comparing things but that historical knowledge really does hang over everything.

NW There you go. Greil Marcus was right all along.

Memory Bucket,
Jeremy Deller, 2004
Video stills

Adrian Street,
Brynmawr, 1974

[5] On 17th February 2001, Manic Street Preachers became the first Western rock'n'roll band to perform in Cuba when they played a one-off show at the Teatro Karl Marx. The gig was witnessed by Fidel Castro.

—

An archive of Jeremy Deller's work can be found at jeremydeller.org

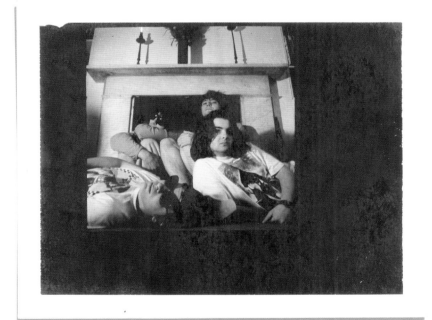

31st Oct, '98 12:57 A.M.
TATTOO M. Hale [?]

5th NOV.'98 9:19 P.M.
M. Ikeda

6th NOV.'98 6:16 P.M.
M. Ikeda

5th Feb '99 5:04 P.M.
REHARSALL

5th Feb '99 5:07 P.M.
REHARSALL

16th MAR. '99 6:11 P.M.
PAST DOICHLAND M.Freda
IN FRANCE

12th MAR. '99 3:21 P.M.
DRESDEN M.Freda

15th MAR. '99 11:58 A.M
TIRED SEAN

15th MAR. '99 12:31 A.M
FAMOUS FACES M.Freda

23rd MAR. '99   12:55 P.M
OLD & NEW   M.J. Reda

24th MAR. '99   3:20 P.M.
HOLLY (SPOKY) M.J. Reda

24th MAR. '99   2:54 P.M.
HOLLY MAN   M.J. Reda

24th MAR. '99   3:25 P.M.
FLASH   M.J. Reda

5th MAR. 199   1:02 P.M.
DANGER XXX   Wolfgang

5th MAR. 199   12:57 P.M
MAN WALKING ON THE RIVER

5th MAR '99 12:36 PM
FRZEN RIVER

5th MAR.'99 12:45 PM
HOUSE IS FUN

25th Feb. '98   11:55 A.M.
ANGEL

9th MAR. '99   1:18 P.M.
TWIN ANGEL

26th Feb. '98   2=15 P.M
MANIC STREET PREACHERS M. Areda

26th Feb. '98 3=19 P.M.
MANIC STREET PREACHERS M. Areda

4th NOV. '98 2:32 P.M.
IL DUMO M. Ikeda

4th NOV. '98 2:04 P.M.
BEAUTIFUL-TOWN M. Ikeda

5th NOV. '98 1:48 P.M.
M. Ikeda

5/11/98 2:03
TREE-SHADOWS M. Ikeda

27th JAN. '99 3:11 P.M.
LOOK-OVER-SEAN M.J.Preda

25th JUNE '99 11:20 A.M.
SUMMER-SEAN M.J.Preda

20th Sep. '98 3:40 P.M.
ON THE BEACH M.J.Preda

11/12/98 9:05 P.M.
S.M. M.J.Preda

25th April '98 3:07 P.M.
(CHILL OUT)
THIS IS K.L.F. M.Ikeda

25th April '98 1:39 P.M
NATURAL M.Ikeda

31st JAN. '99   1:15 P.M.
BLUE SKY (PERTH) M.Ikeda [印]

25th JAN. '99   3:55 P.M.
BEAUTIFUL SKY   M.Ikeda [印]

14th Oct. '98   3:29 P.M.
SNOW MOUNTAIN   M.J.Preda

14th Oct. '98   3:48 P.M
SNOW-COUNTRY   M.J.Preda

14th Oct, '98   2:06 P.M.
THIS IS
MY WAY   M.J.Preda

14/10/98   11:37 A.M.
THE ROAD TO   M.J.Preda
XXXX

14 /10 /98   2:47 P.M.
LANDSCAPE

8th MAY '98 5=50 P.M.
RUMBLE - WIRE

8th MAY '98 8=24
RUMBLE J.D. M.Street

25th Feb. '98   3:07 P. M.
DEAD - GOLD FISH

15th MAY '98   5:22 P.M.
BBC   M.Ikeda

15th MAY '98   5:23 P.M.
BBC   M.Ikeda

23rd JAN '99 11:03 A.M.
SUNNY

12/12/98 3:10 P.M.
GLASGOW

1 / 3 / 99   4:00 P.M.
BOOKEND   M. Ikeda

1 / 3 / 99   4:02 P.M.
WHO   M. Ikeda

1st. MAR.'99   4:18 P.M.
M.Ikeda 印

1st MAR.'99   4:07 P.M
ICE   M.Ikeda 印

20th Sep. '98 1:13 P.M.
MEMORY   M.J.Preda

20th Sep. '98 12:56 P.M.
DEAD REEF   M.J.Preda

20th Sep. '98 12:24 P.M.
SWANSEA   M.J.Preda

21st Sep. '98 1:53 P.M.
SPOOKY TREE M.J.Preda

12th MAR. '99 4:37 P.M.
EX EAST GERMANY M.Ikeda

12th MAR. '99 10:21 A.M.
BERLIN MORRNING M.Ikeda

25th MAR. '99 4:45 P.M.
COLOGNE M.Ikeda

26th MAR. '99 10:24 A.M.
KÖLN M.Ikeda

10th MAR, '99 5:06 P.M.
DEUTCHLAND M.Ikeda

11th MAR. '99 3:07 P.M.
BERLIN M.Ikeda

14th MAR. '99 1:57 P.M
GERMAN FOREST

13th MAR. '99 5:11 P.M.

14 / 9 / 98   11:04 P.M.
J. DEAN B.   M. Ikeda 24

27th Feb. '98 1:12 P.M
DOG~EYES   M. Ikeda 43

17 / 10 / 98   11:10 A.M.
TUNNEL #2   M Ikeda

22nd JAN '99   3:49 P.M.
TREE   M Ikeda

31/10/98   8:38 A.M.
I LOVE SPAIN   M·S·Reda

1st NOV. 98   1:03 P.M.
PINCH + PUNCH
FIRST OF THE MONTH   M·S·Reda

14th OCT. '98 11:43 A.M.
BEAUTFFUL-SILENT M.Speeda

14th OCT. '98 11:58 A.M.
LOTs WATTER M.Speeda

14th Oct, '98 2:38 P.M.
MOORE-SIDE M. Breda

20th AUG '98 5:15 P.M.
CHRISTIANIA M.V Reader

20/8/98 5:14 P.M.
CHRISTIANIA M.V Reader

20th AUG. '98   5:11 P.M.
CHRISTIANIA   M.Ikeda

20 / 8 /98   5:19 P.M
CHRISTIANIA   M.Ikeda

18/9/98   10:42 A.M.
ROAD TO NORTH   M. Ikeda

18/9/98   4:35 P.M.
SCOTLAND   M. Ikeda

18/9/98   4:00 P.M.
M. Ikeda

20th Sep. '98   8:02 P.M.
SWANSEA SUNSET   M. Ikeda

4th NOV. '98   1:42 P.M.
MILAN

7th MAR. '99 11:02 P.M.
SHOW TIME M.Freedom

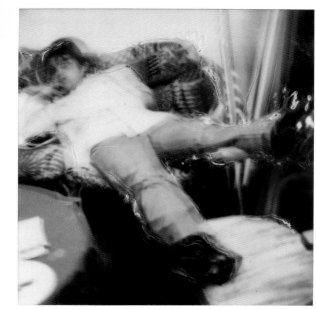

7th MAR. '99 11:58 P.M.
AFTER SHOW

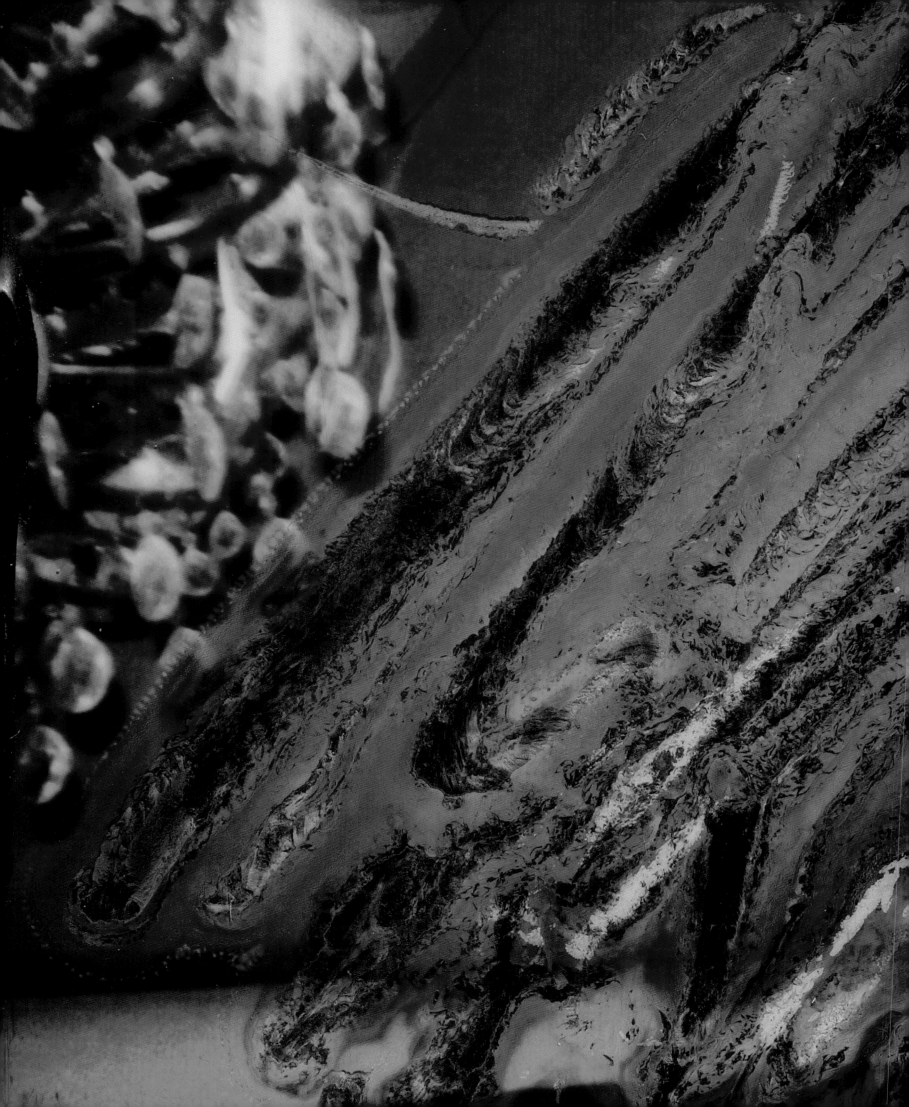

4th MAR, '99 4:02 P.M.
①SWEDISH T.V. M.J.Reck①

4th MAR. '99 4:03 P.M.
CHANNEL ④ M.J.Reck②

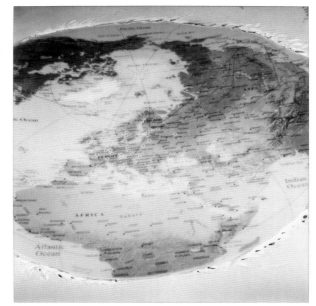

4th MAR. '99 9:37 P.M
FINLAND

5th MAR. '99 8:15 A.M.
HELSINKI

2/ 7 /98   11:52 A.M,
7°-4 WIRE   M. Ikeda

3rd JULY '98 10:43 P.M.
BLIND MAN J.D.B. M. Ikeda

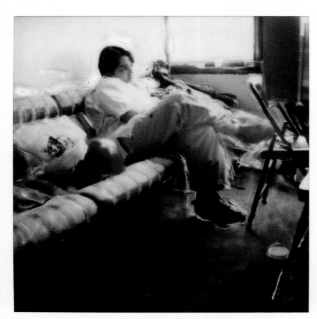

2nd JULY '98 12:31 P.M.
MR. SEAN MOORE M. Ikeda

2/7/98   11:55 A.M.
7°-4 MOORE M. Ikeda

3rd JULY '98   10:17 P.M.
IF YOU TOLERATE... M Preda

3rd JULY '98   10:36 P.M.
MODERN LOVERS   M Preda

23rd Sep.'98 4:46 P.M.
CHESS WIRE M. Ueda

23rd sep. '98   3:38 P.M.
KING MAN CHAIR

16th Sep. '98   6:58 P.M.
FALL   MJIkeda

30th Oct. '98   5:03 P.M.
BEAUTIFFUL-DAY   MJIkeda

17th Oct. '98   8:23 P.M
GOTHENBURG   MJIkeda

5th NOV. '98   2:02 P.M.
BLUE SKY   MJIkeda

1st Nov. '98   3:50 P.M.
LISBON   M.Ikeda

5th NOV. '98   6:47 A.M.
GOOD-MORRNING   M.Ikeda

7th NOV. '98   5:23 P.M.
AMSTERDAM   M.Ikeda

25th JAN '99   12:05
CHINA-TOWN   M.Ikeda

26th Feb. '98   12:24 P.M
SPOOKY MOORE   M.Freda

25th Feb. '98   4:22 P.M.
BEAUTY - WIRE   M.Freda

25th Feb. '98   2:34 P.M.
HULL-WIRE   M.I.Ikeda

25th Feb. '98   1:50 P.M.
SEAN-COLD   M.I.Ikeda

6th MAR. '99 11:21 A.M.
HEL ⇒ STO ⇒ OSL M.Sreda

30th JAN. '99 7:10 P.M.
FLY TO PERTH M.Sreda

24th MAR. '99   2:38 P.M.
POWER   M. Okeda [PB]

24th MAR. '99   2:40 P.M.
HOLLY POWER   M. Okeda [PB]

26th JAN '99   4:10 P.M.
WIRE COOL   MJ Peed

26/1/99   4:11 P.M.
PLAY GAME SEAN

26/1/99   4:11 P.M
JDB + NN   MJ Peed

26th JAN '99   5:30 P.M.
MANICS LIVE   MJ Peed

7:44 A.M.

FREE SOUL   27/2/98
OK M·IKEDA

29th MAR 2001   7:17 p.m.
AT MARRIOTT #2   M J Preda

29th MAR 2001   6:36 p.m.
AT MARRIOTT #1   M J Preda

23rd Oct '98   3:40 P.M.
(FIRE WORK)
STAINED GLASS

27/10/98   9:37 K.M.
GOTHIC

5th Feb. '99 1:40 P.M.

5th Feb '99 1:47 P.M.

5th Feb '99 1:45 P.M.
SNOW TOWN

5th Feb. '99 1:53 P.M.
SNOW MOUNTAIN

171   172

173   174

5th Feb '99   1:51 P.M.
JDB   M. Ikeda [B]

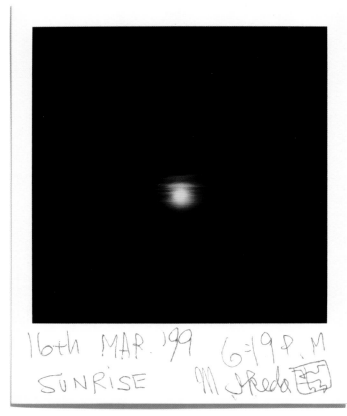

16th MAR. '99   6:19 P. M
SUNRISE   M Freda

16th MAR. '99   6:18 P.M.
WIRE   M Freda

23/9/98   4:08 P.M.
BRUISE   MJPreda

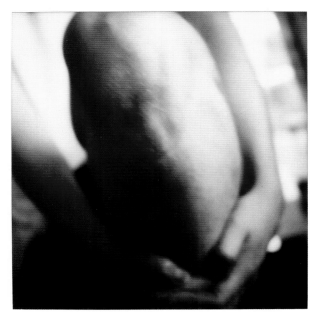

23/9/98   4:09 P.M
BRUISE #2   MJPreda

28th JAN '99 11:39 A.M.
AT AIR PORT M. Preda

30th JAN. '99 2:23 P.M.

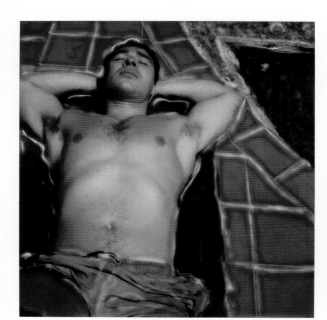

30th JAN.'99 3:02 P.M.
STEAVE M. Preda

29th JAN. '99 8:01 P.M.
JAMES DEAN M. Preda

31st JAN '99 5:45 P.M.
GOOD TIRED M.Streda

30th JAN '99 10:41 A.M.
HUGE SKY M.Streda

31st JAN, '99 11:59 A.M.
AUS. vs SRI. M.Streda

31st JAN. '99 11:47 A.M.
DRINKS TROLLEY M.Streda

3rd Sep. '98   9:07 P.M

WIRE

13th Sep. '98   2:32 P.M.

DYMA'N NGWIRONEDD
 — DWÊD UN TI

30th JAN, '99   3:54 P.M.
SWIM - WIRE

30th JAN, 99   4:04 P.M.
WIRE IN SPA

30th JAN, '99   3:55 P.M.
SWIM -WIRE

31st JAN, '99   2:27 P.M.
COOL J.D.B   Mikech

22nd Oct, '98   11:14 A.M.
BEAUTIFUL (BACK) M. Ikeda

22nd Oct, '98   11:06 A.M.
BEAUTFUL (FRONT) M. Ikeda

26th MAR. '99   11:02A.M
GOD ?   M.Preda

28th MAR. '99   4:30P.M.
PARIS   M.Preda

26th MAR. '99   10:26 A.M.
WHO ?   M.Preda

28th MAR. '99   6:23P.M
FREEDOM   M.Preda

8th MAR.'99   2:28 P.M.
SEAN - LEICA

8th MAR.'99   12:17 P.M
DENMARK AT SEAN

29th JAN '99   12:56 P.M.
ON THE ROAD   M. Redd ⑤

29th JAN '99   12:34 P.M.
JAPANESE LUNCH S.M. M. Redd ⑤

3rd MAR. '99   4:51 P.M.
MR. MARTIN IN JAPANESE FLAG

3rd MAR '99   3:18 P.M.
OLD TOWN

3rd MAR. '99   4:27 P.M
NARROW ALLEY

4th MAR. '99   3:57 P.M.

16 /10/98   2:47 P.M.
M Streda

27th Feb. '98   4:42 P.M.

21st AUG '99   8:24 P.M.
NICKY   M Streda

14th Sep. '98　11:19 P.M.
SEAN MOORE　M.Streda

14th Sep. '98　10:57 P.M.
WIRE　M.Streda

10th MAY '97   2:49P.M.
MR MIRE M.J.Prado [seal]

23/8/97   8:04P.M.
MR.GRUFF M.J.Prada [seal]

14th Sep. '98 12:45 A.M.
JOB   M.J.Prada [seal]

27th April '98 12:42P.M.
NICK NASMYTH   M.J.Prada [seal]

5th FEB, '99   12:58 P.M.
AKIRA   M. Ikeda

5th Feb '99   2:15 P.M.
NOT REAL   M. Ikeda

5th Feb '99   2:4 P.M.
M. Ikeda

5th Feb '99   2:23 P.M
OSAKA BAY   M. Ikeda

10th Feb. '99 11:13 A.M.
GOD TREA

10th Feb. '99 12:42 P.M.
WORKING AROUND
SHINJUKU

25th Feb. '98   12:24 P.M.
MORNING - SEAN PENN

25th Feb. '98   12:43 P.M.
GUITAR - WIRE

25th Feb. '98   3:16 P.M.
J.D.B. HAND+TEA

25th Feb. '98   12:05 P.M.
ORANGES

22nd JAN '99
SYDNEY

22nd JAN '99 2:55 P.M.
DON JOHNSON HEAD

23rd JAN '99 11:49 A.M.
SEAN IN SIDNEY

23rd JAN '99 5:45 P.M.
SYDNEY FUN

25th JAN '99   5:23 P.M.
CITY

27th JAN. '99   3:26 P.M.
TOP OF TOWER

23rd JAN '99   11:47 A.M
SIDNEY SKY

27th JAN. '99 3:17 P.M.
RIALTO VISON THEATRE

4th DEC, '98   7:40 A.M.

17th AUG '98   4:49 P.M.
KING OF ROCK

31st JAN. '99   2:25 P.M.
J.D.B. EYES

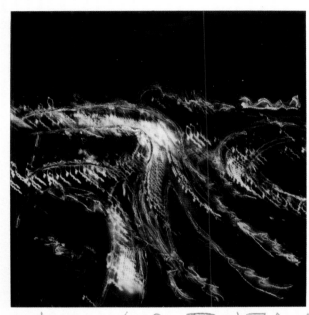

31/10/98 3:17 A.M.
FUCK'N'NIGHT

18/9/98   10:44 A.M
ROAD TO NORTH   M.Preda

17th Oct. '98   10:57 A.M.
SNOWING NORWAY   M.Preda

7th NOV. '98   2=04 P.M.
FLAT   MJReda 西

7th NOV. '98   2:09 P.M.
PROPERA   MJReda 西

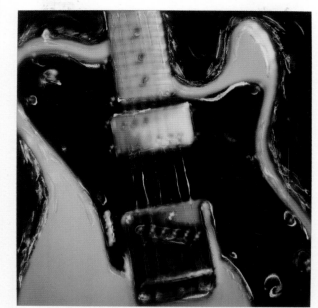

26th April '98 12:36 P.M.
1974 TELECASTER M.J.Preda

27th Feb. '98 12:07 P.M.
DARK-SIDE-OF
THE-MOON M.J.Preda

26th April '98 3=21 P.M.
HEAD-PHONE M.Ikeda

26th April '98 12=29 A.M.
DAVE ERINGAK M.Ikeda

1st. MAR. '99   7j:22 P.M

DRUM SET   M. Ikeda

1st. MAR. '99　8:47 P.M.
SEAN　M Ikeda

1st. MAR. '99　8:51 P.M.
NICKY WIRE　M Ikeda

1st. MAR. '99　8:56 P.M.
BLUR SEAN

1st. MAR. '99　8:43 P.M.
JDB　M Ikeda

255　256

257　258

26th JAN '99 8:11 P.M
MJIkeda

3rd JULY '9   3=15 P.M.
MASKS   MJIkeda

11/11/98   5:13 P.M
JEVIL TOOSE M.(fecla A)

19/12/98   3:40 P.M
EXETER

25th April '98   1:32 P.M.
BEAUTIFUL   ✓   Ikeda [2/3]

25th April '98   1:21 P.M.
BLUE SKY   M. Ikeda [4/3]

26th April '98   1:40 P.M
LION-WIRE #1   M.Jfresh 4/3

26th April '98   1:41 P.M.
LION-WIRE #2   M.Jfresh 4/3

19/12/98
EXETER   3·37 P.M.
                M.Reed

12/12/98   2:42 P.M.
MANCHESTER   M.Reed

10/12/98
SHEFFIELD

9th DEC '98   11:52 A.M.
BOURNEMOUTH   Mishima

20/9/98   12:47 P.M.
SWANSEA   Mishima

5th MAR. '99 3:10 P.M.
INTERVIEWS (PRESS)

13th AUG. '98 6:16 P.M.
MSP REHASALLING

1st MAR. '99   2:38 P.M
STOCKHOLM   M.Ikeda

1st MAR. '99 3:30 P.M
WINDOW'S VEW   M.Ikeda

1st MAR. '99   3:45 P.M.
M.Ikeda

1st MAR. '99   4:05 P.M.
VAIKING SHIP   M.Ikeda

6th MAR '99   11:51 A.M
OSLO   M. Ikeda [B]

13th MAR. '99   5:06 P.M.
M. Ikeda [P]

23rd April '98 11:55 P.M.
NICK PLAY B.G. M.J Prada

2/7/98   5:47 P.M.
SPACE - WIRE   M.J Prada

26th JAN '99   8:15 P.M.
BLUR - WIRE   M.J Prada

2nd JULY '98 11:30 A.M.
GUCCI WIRE   M.J Prada

13th AUG. '98   6:18 P.M.
MSP REHASALING

25th JAN '99   4:23 P.M.
REHARSAL

7th Feb. '99   7:13 P.M.
LIVE (GREAT)

6th NOV. '98   7:15 P.M.
REHASSAL

6th MAR. '99 5:36 P.M.
SNOWLAND   M. Ikeda

8th MAR. '99   8:49 A.M.
DENMARK

21st JAN. '99   2:42 P.M.
CHINESE-MOORE   M. Streda

23rd JAN '99   1:51 P.M.
WIRE'S ROOM   M. Streda

21/1/99   2:43 P.M
30 YEARS NICKY   M. Freeda [F]

21/1/99   2:43 P.M.
IN DOWN UNDER   [H]

27th Feb. '98   6:39 P.M.

27th Feb. '98   6:14 P.M.
POWER-PLAY J.D.B.

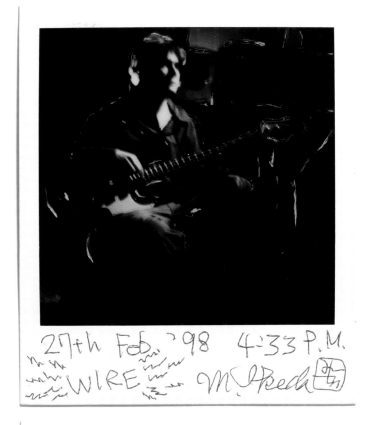

27th Feb '98   4:33 P.M.
WIRE   M. Ikeda

27th Feb '98   4:27 P.M.
BASSMENT   M. Ikeda

25th JAN.'99   5:03 P.M.
HOT MELTING   M.Ikeda

19th Oct, '98   1:29 P.M.
ROAD TO LUND   M.Ikeda

25th JUNE '99 3:02 P.M.
JOHN LENON-WIRE

25th JUNE '99 1:44 P.M.
NEW STICK

19th MAR. '99   3:02 P.M.
GAUDI GHOST   MJ Reda

19th MAR. '99   3:25 P.M.
GOD BLESS YOU   MJ Reda

21st MAR.) 99   12-45 P.M.
BULL ON THE HILL   M Welch '88

304

20th Oct. '98   7:30 P.M.
DENMARK   M J Reda

23rd Oct, '98   9:31 A.M.
HAMBURG   M J Reda

24th Oct, '98   3:22 P.M.
BERLIN

25th Oct, '98   11:30 A.M.
RAIN

11/12/98   9:04 P.M.
N.W.

11/12/98   9:03 P.M
J.D.B.

13/12/98   12:38 P.M.
QUODRPHENIA

16/10/98   2:56 P.M.

Znd NOV '98   3:13 P.M
SIGNING

23rd April '98   7:17 P.M.
DINNER   M. Pfreda

23th April '98 7:12 P.M.
MONNOW VALLEY STUDIO M. Areda

17th Oct. '98   10:42 A.M
NORWAY   M.Freda

17/10/98   10:53 A.M
TUNNEL 1   M.Freda

14/10/98   1:57 P.M.
WHERE WE
GOING xxxx   M.Freda

29th AUG. '98 11:32 A.M.
ROAD TO SLANE   M.Freda

18th MAR. '99   12:35 P.M.
SPAIN

16th MAR. '99   6:31 P.M.
SUN ALLWAYS SAME

16th MAR. '99   6:17 P.M.
BEAUTIFULLAND

16th MAR. '99   6:29 P.M.
FLY TO HEAVEN

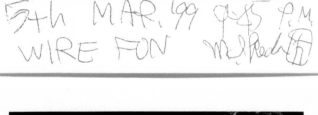

5th MAR. '99 9:45 P.M.
WIRE FUN m.Ikeda

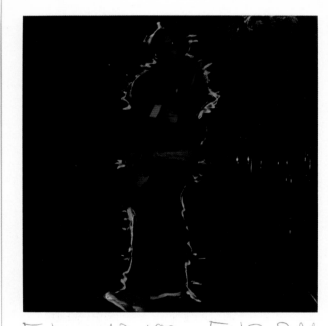

5th MAR. '99 5:13 P.M.
LIVE WIRE m.Ikeda

5th MAR. '99 5:08 P.M.
W/RE M.J. Fresh [?]

12/12/98   3:55 P.M.
GLASGOW   MJFreda

12/12/98   3:50 P.M.
GLASGOW   MJFreda

24th JUNE '99   3:21 P.M.
$ HAPPY   M.Ikeda

3rd Sep. '98   9:20 P.M.
FLY J.D.B.   M.Ikeda

27th JAN '99 4:21 P.M.

DOG

26th April '98   2:37 P.M.
IDLE EUROPEAN

26th April '98   2:43 P.M.
SOUND~D   M. Peach圖

14th. Sep '98 12:49 A.M.
SIGNING   M.J Prada

9th NOV. '98 8:34 P.M.
VISA PICTUERS M.J Prada

25th Feb '98   7:02 P.M.
NICKY WIRE

26th April '98   3=15 P.M.
???? J.D.B.

26th Feb. '98   1:20 P.M
SUPER – MOORE

27th Feb. '98   12:58 P.M
JAMES DEAN

25th Feb '98 6:55 P.M.
SEAN MOORE M. Ikeda

22nd Feb '98 12:05 P.M.
SELF-JAMES

25th Feb. '98   1:27P.M
BLUR-WIRE

25th Feb. '98   12:00P.M.
GENIUS MIKE

21st AUG. '99   7:41 P.M

JDB   M. Peda 🖊

21st AUG '99   7:37 P.M.

SEAN   M. Peda 🖊

21st AUG '99   7:46 P.M

WIRE

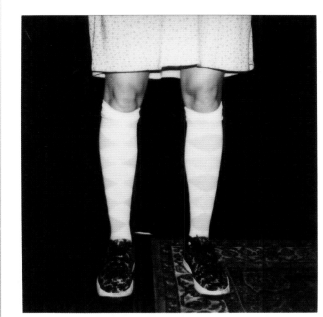

21st AUG '99   7:50 P.M

θ=39

θ=40

17/2/2001
OLD TOWN #5

17th Feb 2001
OLD TOWN #1

17th Feb 2001
OLD TOWN #6

17th Feb 2001
O.T. #2

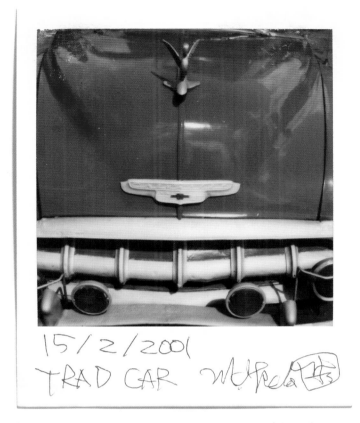

15/2/2001
TRAD CAR

17/2/2001
OLD TOWN #4

15th Feb, 2001 3:19 P.M.
CUBA SEA

16th Feb, 2001 3:09 P.M
AFTER PRESS CON, N. SKY

18th Feb. 2001
Che-COUNTRY   M.Ikeda

16th Feb 2001   7:00 A.M.
CUBA
MORRNING   M.Ikeda

18th Feb 2001
EAYS SO BEAUTFULL

18th Feb 2001
CUBAN SKY   M.Preda

18th Feb 2001
SAD   M.Preda

18th Feb 2001
che close

18th Feb 2001
che GUN

15/2/2001
NICK & SEAN

15th Feb 2001
REVORUTION PARK

15/2/2001
WALKING TO ~~CHE~~
GEBARA

15th Feb 2001 5:31 P.M
QUBA FLAG

27th JAN. '99 4:18 P.M.
FLOWER AUS.

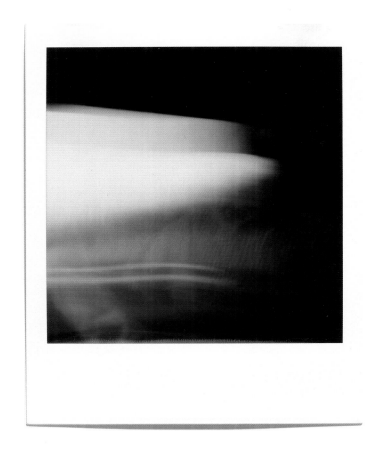

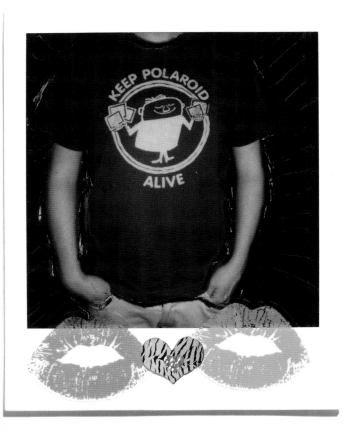

Black Holes

390

SOCIALIST SERENADE

IF YOU Decode this THEN YOUR CHildRENWill Be NExiT

BLACK DOG. ON MY SHOULDER

READY FOR DROWNING

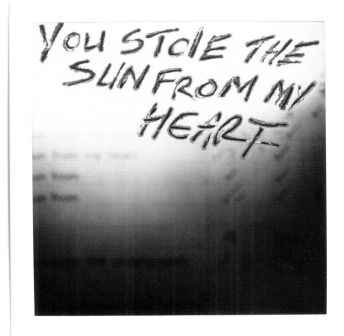

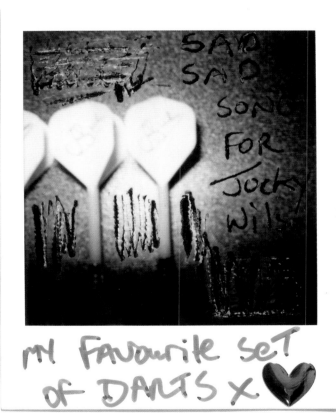

DOUGLAS ♥
J. Collins

film shoot ⭐

① PEELED APPLES ✓
② PRETENSION/REPULSION ✓
③ FACING PAGE TOP LEFT ✓
④ Jackie Collins Existential Q-Time ✓
⑤ WILLIAMS LAST WORDS ✓
⑥ MARION JO ✓
⑦ VIRGINIA STATE Epileptic Colony ✓
⑧ BAG LADY ✓
⑨ DOORS CLOSING SLOWLY ✓
⑩ THIS JOKE SPORT SEVERED ✓
⑪ SHE BATHED HERSELF IN A BATCH ✓
⑫ JOURNAL FOR PLAGUE LOVERS ✓
⑬ ME AND STEPHEN HAWKING ✓
⑭ ALL IS VANITY ✓
FINISH JAN 31st

CARDIFF STUDIO

413   414

415   416

421   422

423   424

427   428

429   430

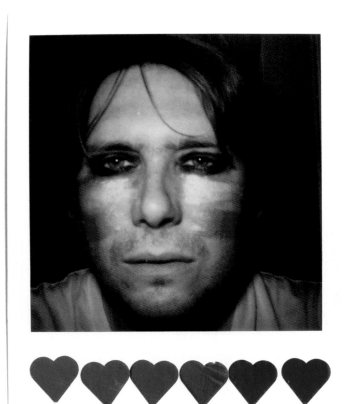

455   456

461

463

464

465   466

467   468

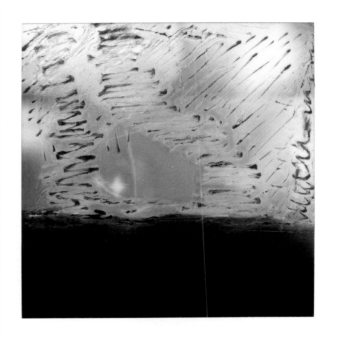

forever

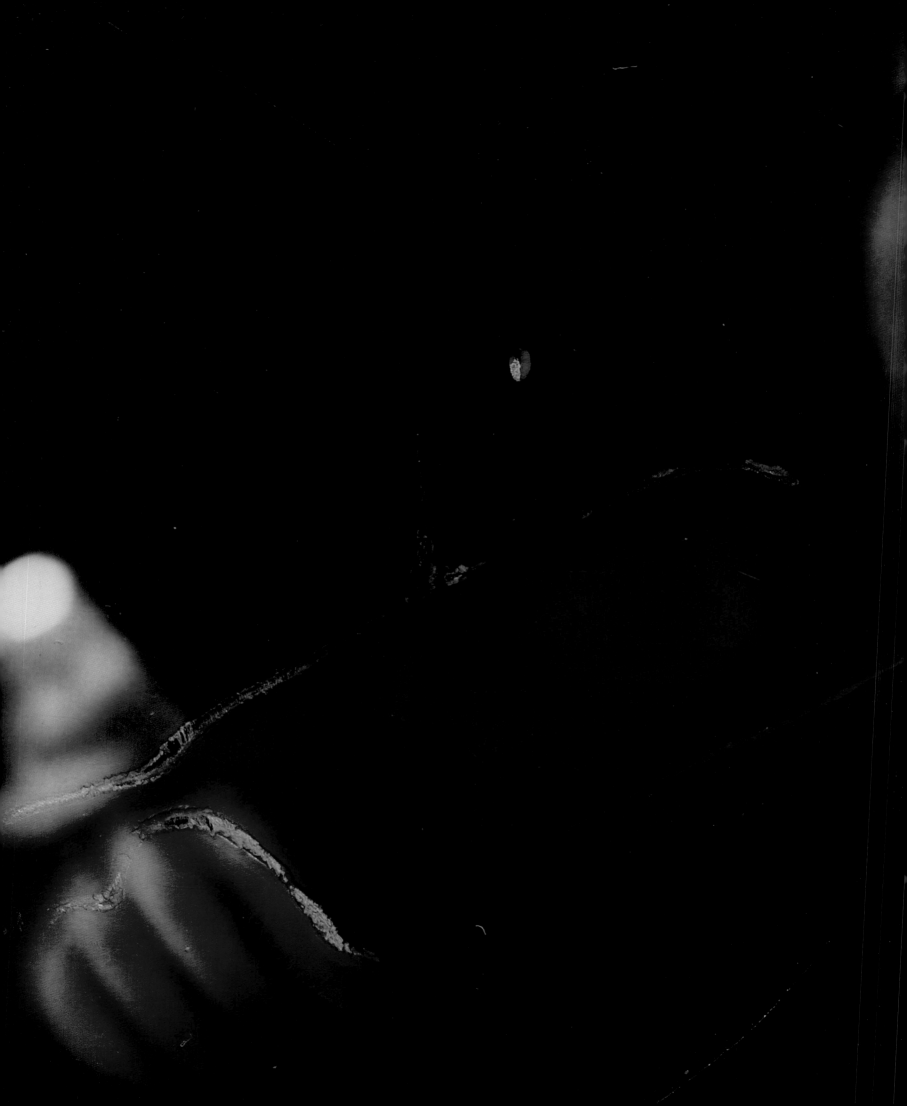

475

476

483 484

485 486

487   488

489   490

491

492

495   496

497   498

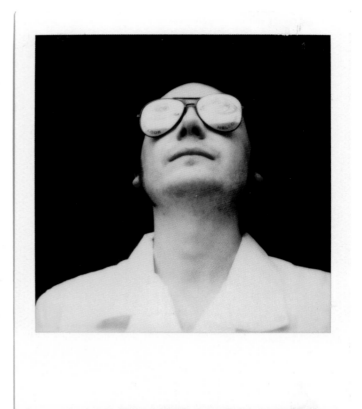

501   502

503   504

522

523

526   527

528   529

530   531

532   533

x LoZ x

MY LITTLE EMPIRE

BLACKHOLES for the Young

REFLECTIONS –
R·S·THOMAS

SOUTH YORKSHIRE MASS MURDERER
SYMM

Tell ME YOURS

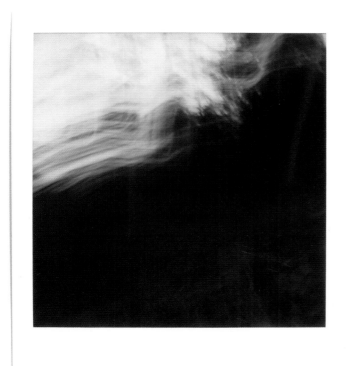 

Commentary
Nicky Wire

These images are test shots taken at the start of magazine photo sessions. The Polaroids were always given to me by the photographer; I kept them as mementos ever since, always thinking that someday they'd be good to link together somehow. Some of the sessions I vividly remember, some are very foggy. I think these images give a good, broad sweep – certainly of the early years, back at the point where we were properly becoming a band. There's everything from Mitch's first session with us through to one of the much-missed Biscuit Tin from *Smash Hits*. Kevin Cummins's shots for our first cover of the *NME* right through to our first *Q* cover with Rankin. For me, it's a reminder that over the years we've worked with some truly brilliant photographers.

There's something really innately charming about these shots – something innocent, prior to starting to pose for the proper shots. There's a couple of iconic shots taken by Tom Sheehan for the *Melody Maker* [011/012]. Bizarrely, at a gig in Wolverhampton this year (May 2011), I met a girl outside the venue who had the actual shirt on – stencilled with 'Dead Flowers' with the Marilyn Monroe postcard stuck to it. She'd bought it on eBay. I remember giving it away way back in the day and it obviously ended up for sale many years later. She came on the bus with her mum, they'd won a competition to meet us that ran with the *Postcards* album. They'd made us a load of Manic Street Preachers cupcakes.

The thing I really like about this section is the variation on the format. About 95 per cent of the rest of the book is shot on the classic Polaroid 600 film. But here you've got variation, based on what the photographer was working with. There's an amazing Kevin Cummins one that was taken during the *Gold Against the Soul* campaign; it's a large-format picture where you peel away the backing and you're left

with something like an imprint, a ghost of a picture almost [010].

On all of those early photo sessions, we would go in with a very strong idea of how we wanted to present ourselves. The idea we had for the first *NME* cover [002] was for me and Richey to go out and get ourselves covered in love bites. I'm pretty sure it was the first time they had done a cover without using either the whole band or the singer. Sticking the bass player and the non-playing guitarist on a band's first front cover seems a pretty radical idea, even now. I remember it was a real thrill to meet Kevin Cummins back then as we'd grown up idolising his classic pictures of Joy Division, The Smiths and the Bunnymen. There was no problem from James and Sean about it going that way.

The first shot in the book – the *Holy Bible* one – I think it's by Neil Cooper. It's such a brilliant shot and sets the tone for the whole of that era – the military gear, that whole sober, sombre mood that pervaded everything around then. Just before that stage [013], there's a really interesting picture that Steve Gullick took for the *Melody Maker*. That was the gold-paint session, there are other pictures from the same session [008/009] taken before we took our clothes off. They were taken just before we recorded *The Holy Bible*; I think it was for 'Life Becoming a Landslide' coming out as a single. These were the days when you'd still get a magazine cover for the fourth single off an album. We'd started using the camouflage at that point, the military gear on stage. There's something spectral – troubled almost – about the picture of the band [013]. Almost lost looking. I find it quite disturbing to look at now. Sean in particular looks just . . . so odd.

Around that same time, there's a shot [014] that was taken for the much-missed *Select* magazine. That

was for a special porn issue. I look truly nuts. The rest of the session got a lot worse. There's one where I was just scratching at my pubes. Horrible.

There's a few [006/007] that were taken from a cover shoot by Mitch Ikeda for *Rockin' On* magazine in Japan. It was our first time over there. For them to put a band on their first album on the cover was a massive thing. We'd met Mitch previously in the UK but that was the first time he'd shot us properly – it was a truly epic session. There are a few others [019–021] that were taken by Mitch where he wanted to make us look like Lawrence of Arabia – T. E. Lawrence of course being Welsh . . .

There's a couple [017/018] that are just lovely. I can't remember for the life of me who took them, where they came from even. It was for either *The Independent* or *The Guardian*. The session took place in Phillip (Hall) and Terri's house. In a Welsh way, we're all cwtching up together. Philip and Terri would be out all day and we would just be there hanging around. Those pictures sum up that early stage of the band; they're a tender reflection of a band that's just moved to London and is still bonding.

Later on, there are some pictures from the time that Richey was in hospital [024/025] when we were promoting *The Holy Bible*. They're particularly stark shots; just of James and me.

I can really remember the circumstances surrounding another of Tom Sheehan's shots [022]. I'd pulled the ligaments in my shoulder and we were booked to do *Later* for the first time ever. This was after *Everything Must Go* had come out; it was a really big thing for a band like us. The arm you can see in shot, I'd stretched it over to pick up the phone in the hotel room and a ligament had just popped and snapped. We ended up getting Pete Townshend's bass player to play instead of me. I'm wearing my pyjama bottoms in the photos. I stayed in the Marriott in Regent's Park for five days getting therapy. It makes me sad to think it took that long to get on *Later* . . . everything comes so fast to bands these days. They made bands like us fucking work for it! And it's a real shame that we never played the show with Richey.

There are quite a few shots taken by Rankin from a number of different sessions [026-035]. There's a *Q* cover shoot around *Know Your Enemy* and shots from the session for the cover of *Everything Must Go*. I really like Rankin; he always made us feel very comfortable. The best thing a photographer can do is attempt to make the subject feel comfortable within their vision. Rankin always did that. He's just a real chap. I think his images really sum up that whole time; our most successful period saleswise really is defined by him.

The shots by Valerie Phillips are from the run-up to *Send Away the Tigers* [040-042]. You can tell we've rediscovered some kind of muse. After the uptightness of *Know Your Enemy* and *Lifeblood*, they're relaxed in a brilliant way. Valerie is a very naturalistic photographer; I think she got us just right at that point. Slightly insane-looking and very probably thinking, 'Fuck it'.

These shots [043-048] are really interesting. You can tell how much money was being spent in the nineties as the Polaroid format being used is spectacularly expensive. I've never seen one of these 10x8-size prints being used before or since; they're reproduced here actual size. These are all taken in North Wales at Black Rock Sands near Porthmadog, by Andy Earl; they're tests for the artwork for *This Is My Truth, Tell Me Yours*. One that I particularly love [047] is after we jumped over a fence into a private house after seeing a giant rhododendron bush in the garden. There is an amazing quality to all the shots – they are the truest representation of the moment for me. I look at these pictures and I can still taste the ice cream from the van that was parked there; I can smell the fish and chips that we bought after the session.

Mitch Ikeda's Polaroids of the band are so numerous – the section so vast and expansive – it's nearly impossible to pick out specifics. His documentation stretched to painstakingly labelling every single shot with a comment, a time and a date. He would label each one himself and the comments are often beautifully naïve. Sometimes they're oddly spelt but more often than not, they are incredibly incisive. He's formulating his ideas into English and getting something that's occasionally hilarious without him realising it. The titles are brilliantly oblique – 'German Forest', 'Sunny', 'Road to North'. Often there's literally nothing else to say. I love the one that he's captioned 'God?' [196]. Mitch's captions say more than I can.

Mitch's photos achieve a very real intimacy. I can't think of anyone else that we would have allowed into our headspace for so long and let become so involved. He put great care into each shot, I think he thought of each shot – however abstract – as being as important as a posed band shot. The live stuff he shot – it's so hard to get the light right with a Polaroid yet he just nailed it time and again. Life has become so technical – photography especially so. Have you got the right lens, the right lighting, whatever? He's there in the photo pit firing off Polaroids. It just shows perfectly what you can achieve with slender margins. There's lots of great stuff with the fans that achieve a brilliant intimacy. The first of his pictures in here is a great shot of the girl with the *Generation Terrorists* tattoo [049]. There's nothing voyeuristic about it, it's just a totally pure reflection of proper fandom.

Mitch's relationship with us properly began around the time he did the *Rockin' On* shoot [006/007]. He took the cover for *Gold Against the Soul* after that. Because of our rock classicism, we'd always been looking for our Pennie Smith (specifically her relationship with The Clash), someone who would perfectly document everything for us. We were always looking to make those sorts of connections and collaborations. In the early days, Mitch's inability to communicate properly in English became an advantage – he was so physical and emotive that he just connected with us perfectly. He is also a brilliant masseur, something that helped get me through so many tours. The pictures of me covered in bruises [178/179] were taken after I'd smashed myself up on stage. After taking the pictures, he gave me the most incredible massage that totally sorted me out.

I kind of pushed him to use the Polaroid more. I felt it was important to have something instant and visceral. I've got thousands of his pictures that he took on other cameras – all printed luxuriously – but it's these pictures I love the most. They have a different kind of soul. By the end of the period, he would be wearing a Polaroid camera around his neck constantly. By then, he'd bought into my love of the colour the pictures produce too.

With the pictures in this book in particular, you can see him making a photographic travelogue of everything we did; from *Everything Must Go* through to Cuba. In every circumstance, from Mike Hedges' studio in France to the video shoot for *Tolerate* [135-140] to us meeting Castro, he was there. There are some amazing photos taken out of plane windows, there are pictures from cities all around the world – his visions of Glasgow or Milan . . . Germany, Australia. There's a whole section that he took in Cuba too which is just utterly glorious. He captures the beautiful neon loneliness of Japan so artfully too. I guess the travelogue element of Mitch's photos reflects how big we were getting. The size of the tours,

the sheer distances we were covering.

There's a cast of characters represented in his pictures, all of the people around us during that time. Steve Head (who ran our security), Mike Hedges, Dave Eringa, Chris Griffiths who tour managed us back then . . . there's a lovely one of Gruff Rhys showing off his beautiful Welsh smile [215] – the Super Furries supported us a good few times back then.

The view through Mitch's lens is in many ways what you see as a band touring; alien views of different cities, often bleary-eyed through jet lag. The woozy view of life on a bus. When we started out, like all bands we had a romanticised view of foreign travel that came from early Simple Minds records – places you'd only ever really imagined, no real concept of what they'd be like. I think that was infectious when Mitch came on board. I love the jumps it makes too. You find yourself jumping from Sydney to Exeter and it makes total sense.

He became a true documenter during that period. It does sometimes seem a little slanted towards me and Sean. Everywhere we stopped off, Sean would hoof it off to see whatever sights there were – the Sydney Harbour Bridge or the remains of the Berlin Wall or the Gaudi buildings in Barcleona. Mitch would always tag along with him and catch him whenever they stopped for a second.

It's interesting to see where he starts to fuck around with the format, scratching and subtly altering the pictures during the development stage. I absolutely love the pair labelled 'Oranges' and 'J.D.B. Hand+Tea' [226/227]. 'Oranges' is like something by an Old Master, it's almost the perfect still life.

Cuba could almost have been a book on its own. Mitch was there when I had my freak-out and started wearing a dress in my room [368/369]

– it was me trying to escape what was going on around us in whatever way I could. I love the look of those pictures. That was what my dad would call a 'funny half-hour'. The ones in Havana, you properly get the feel of what the place was like. The Communist brutalism of it all. It's very much like the Southbank in the sunshine. Somehow the concrete has grown into the landscape, so much so that it's almost more naturalistic than the buildings of the old town.

I think Mitch's dedication to the form had an influence on me. When he became so involved in shooting Polaroid for us, I stopped taking pictures of the band and started concentrating on landscapes and details. It was always such a relief to have him on the bus with mountains of exposed film on him. He even used to take the empty film cartridge, label the box and reinsert the pictures so they became little holders for that particular set of pictures. Mitch's collected Polaroids are a magnificent body of work. They're entirely different from the work collected in his *Forever Delayed* book (which I also absolutely love). The intimacy he achieves here . . . truly these pictures are captured memories.

295

One of the revealing things about the last section – which is the world seen through my amateur eye – is the insight into how the format itself inspires me lyrically. Certain pictures have inspired lyrics, gone on to be single covers or pieces of album artwork. Lots were taken or used around *This Is My Truth*; there are pictures that made up single sleeves or eventually formed the booklet. And there's a lot from my solo album, *I Killed the Zeitgeist*. The simplicity of the format really is an inspirational thing for me to use. Some of the shots have fragments of lyrics or song titles written on them. Not all of them ended up meaning anything but in many cases they acted as triggers. A particular photograph – for example 'Socialist Serenade' [394] – would inspire a mood that would affect the lyrics massively. There's a beautiful photo for 'Nobody Loved You' [400] that's a visual reference to the cherry blossom tree mentioned in the lyrics. In that case I'm not sure which came first. Sometimes the inspiration is very literal. Sometimes the photograph shaped the lyric and sometimes the photograph is an illustration of the lyric.

Some of the pictures taken around the time of *I Killed the Zeitgeist* have been run through my old manual typewriter. They've been scratched, stickered, defaced, adorned. The malleability of a Polaroid – the ability to fuck with the picture and let it process itself – is really quite amazing. Without the technical know-how of someone working in a darkroom or even of someone working in Photoshop, the ability to manipulate the form is incredible.

I love the fact that it's very easy to take pictures of yourself too; that led to lots of self-portraits. I really like the ones I took around *Zeitgeist* [427-434]. I was taking inspiration from Francis Bacon's triptychs; trying to create

a feeling of repetition through subtle differences. It's just me in my bedroom raiding my make-up box and making a record cover out of it. The whole of the solo record – the recordings, the artwork, everything – was extremely minimal. It's as indie as you can get.

Talking specifics, there are a couple of shots [419-420] that, although not the greatest pictures ever taken, are relevant and really interesting because they're the only pictures I've got of *The Holy Bible* recording sessions. I took the one of Sean, Silva and James and I'm not sure whether Richey or Sean took the one of me. They are the last document of Big Noise Recorders in Cardiff where we made the record. They're really snapshots of the recording, a moment showing a group of friends working together. It doesn't really even matter what we looked like in there, the feeling is instant. You just remember why you were there, what it was like.

I think some of the earliest are the ones shot in a bluebell meadow in South Wales [550-551]. That was the point where I started to see the possibilities of the format, where I wanted to start experimenting taking pictures. I used to just wander round where I lived looking at the landscape through the lens, trying to capture thoughts or moments. From there, I became obsessive about the purity of the way landscapes are represented. The colours, the atmosphere. The fact you get shadow, light, mood . . . the fact that they are hardly ever sharply focused and yet the colours are so vivid. There's also something glorious about the way that Polaroid photos capture the snow; they seem to perfectly represent the way that light hits snow [453-456/475-478].

The black-and-white Polaroid is a rare beast indeed but the few that I took are very precious to me. The pictures are mainly from when I lived in Wattsville, back at the first house I lived in with Rachel.

You'd walk out the back of the terrace and you'd be straight in the forest, purely and utterly at one with nature. I can't think of any other way I'd want to capture that time, that place and that memory than with the right batch of black-and-white Polaroid film. There is something so typical of the Valleys in the pictures [437-438] where someone has dumped a fridge up in one of the most beautiful spots in the entire world. It was such a beautiful area to live, I never wanted to leave – and probably wouldn't have – but I was outed from there. After *Everything Must Go* a newspaper printed a story saying "Why Is a Pop Star Living Here?" with a picture of my old miner's terraced house. And that was it; we were rumbled.

Some pictures became part of larger canvases [447-452] that were painted around the time of *This Is My Truth*. The pictures were embedded into the painting – that's why the edges are coloured like they are. For years, Mark Farrow thought he'd lost them but they turned up somewhere in his studio just when we were compiling the book. The artwork was based around the song 'The Everlasting'. In each of them there's a sense of chaos and scratchiness juxtaposed against the stillness of a landscape.

A couple of shots were taken on tour in Japan around the time of *Gold Against the Soul* [425-426]. The most remarkable thing about those pictures is that I look like I might even be enjoying myself, which is rare! The top one is everyone – crew, record label, everyone we were with.

There are a lot of beautiful pictures from Mike Hedges' place in Domfront in Normandy. It's where we recorded about 90 per cent each of *Everything Must Go* and *This Is My Truth*. It was an old place – a château – that he'd converted into a studio. The studio and the village it was in were very typically French

[481-482]. I would wander around the town, snapping away, while James would be playing guitars. The studio has gone now; he had to get rid of it. That's true of most of the places we've ever recorded. Whitfield Street, Wessex, Big Noise obviously . . . all gone now. Thank God we've got our own place in Cardiff. There's a picture of Mike's crappy Citroën [480]. You see the glorious studio he had built – this guy who'd produced legendary and huge records by, The Banshees, The Cure, The Beautiful South . . . then he'd be driving around in a shitty car that would barely ever even work.

Latterly, I documented a lot during the recording of *Journal for Plague Lovers* while we were living down in Rockfield. The only person missing there is Steve Albini and I don't know why. It certainly wasn't because he wouldn't have one taken; he would have been fine about it, he was a total gent. That's a little bit of a regret now.

There could well be a couple of my wife's photos in this collection [510-511] . . . possibly. They're a different size – possibly they were part a photography qualification she was doing. I love them anyway. Such vibrant and pure colours.

There's the most amazing blue sky up on the mountain behind Wattsville [530-533]. There, you can see the Nicky Wire idea of perfection – on a beautiful autumn day, I was walking up there with my dog Molly, on a really long walk up the mountain. There had been some deforesting and the whole place looked like it was on fire; blazing colours everywhere. There's a picture inside the house in Wattsville where Molly was looking out the window, barking at anyone who came past [552].

Probably the final place I got to with Polaroids was taking photographs of other people's pictures of us then defacing them [495-500]. I ended up with a gallery of alternate versions of my favourite band shots from over the years – my own tribute to those pictures in a way.

The more I look at my pictures collected in this last section, the more I think I'm giving away . . . there are so many memories embedded in the pictures, mental snapshots of specific times and places, intimate moments and faded recollections. Things I'd forgotten, things that are burnt in as if they happened minutes ago. And I truly dread to think about the amount of money that's been spent between Mitch and myself on film over the years. When I started it was around £18 for a double pack of films, which was twenty shots. By the end, after they'd stopped producing, you could be looking at around £80 to £100 on eBay for the right stock. It's terrifying really! If I had never picked up the habit, I'd probably be a rich man right now.

Acknowledgements

Thanks to James, Sean and Richey; Robin for making it all happen; Mam and Dad for their Polaroid family albums; Mitch Ikeda for his patience and dedication; Rachel for her photos and expertise; Polaroid film for its simplicity and beauty; Mark Farrow, Gary Stillwell and all at Farrow Design; Lee Brackstone and all at Faber & Faber.

The photos in the first section [001-048] were all donated to Nicky Wire by the photographers at various band sessions between 1991 and 2007. To all the photographers whose pictures feature – heartfelt thanks for the gifts of beautiful and inspirational Polaroids from all of those magical sessions.